Dragon's Tail For Sale

Mark J. Beasley

Illustrations by
Kem Welch

Mark J. Beasley

Illustrated by Kem Welch
Produced by Publish Pros | publishpros.com

Acknowledgments

Kem Welch — For his continued creativity and illustrating know-how. His contribution to this project surpasses anything I could have dreamed of.

Laura Schwarz — Her support and collaboration throughout this effort is incalculable.

Erika Nein — Her editing prowess in addressing key issues is greatly appreciated.

Rich Carnahan — For his benevolent efforts in bringing this manuscript together for publication.

Contents

Dragon's Tail for Sale

I've got a dragon's tail for sale,
It's scaley, long, and green.
It's surely the most wretched tail
Of any dragon ever seen.

It's twenty feet from end to end
When it's lying on the floor.
But I can't wait to get rid of this thing,
So I don't see it anymore.

It's hard to haul this tail around,
That's why it's up for sale.
It's big and heavy, fat and round,
Like every dragon's tail.

I've got a dragon's tail for sale
That's cumbersome and large.
It also comes with a fifty-foot dragon,
Of course, at no extra charge.

I'll Be There Before the Bell

I'll be riding on a rocket
All the way to school.
I guess I'll be the first to break
The *Do Not Ride a Rocket* rule.

I figured I needed a personal rocket
After I studied the situation.
The technology and all my know-how
Provides the perfect combination.

I just walked into the rocket store
On Propulsion Avenue,
Handed over my hard-earned money,
And that's all I had to do.

All the funding for this project
Was well thought-out and planned.
It all came from sufficient donations,
And, of course, my lemonade stand.

Now, what you see before you
Is a marvel of engineering,
With state-of-the-art technology
And calibrated steering.

The aerodynamic titanium frame
Makes the structure perfectly stable.
The interior elements are all connected
By an intertwining cable.

The Acme modified oxidizer
Is a component I can trust,
And the computer automatically calculates
The right amount of thrust.

The gyroscope is functional
And the radar, activated.
The cutting-edge propulsion systems
Are quite sophisticated.

I've mapped out my trajectory
And sequenced the navigation.
These sentinel-like sensors detect
Any shift in orientation.

Yes I was late for school this week
And many times before,
But after I fire up this thing,
That won't happen anymore.

I've cleared the pad for launching
And as far as I can tell,
I can almost guarantee,
I'll be there before the bell.

I'm going to get to school on time,
No matter what it takes.
I just need to figure out
Where they put the brakes!

Pogo Sticks

Come gather 'round,
You poor kangaroos,
And listen to a bit
Of exciting news.

Now pay attention
To what I'm announcing:
These pogo sticks
Are great for bouncing!

I've got pogo sticks
For sale at a price
That you can't pass up,
So don't think twice.

Just step right up
And do some shopping.
Then climb aboard
And do some hopping.

I brought in a load
From Osaka, Japan,
And I need to sell them
As fast as I can.

These pogo sticks
For kangaroos
Are the perfect thing
For you to use.

If you buy one now,
I'll guarantee
A year of service
That's maintenance free.

Just make payments
That you can afford,
Because prices like these
Cannot be ignored.

It's the deal of a lifetime!
There's no time to lose!
Get 'em while they last,
You poor kangaroos.

I'd Rather Have a Root Canal

I've compiled a list of items
That I eat without remorse,
Like sausage links and pancakes
And scrambled eggs, of course.

I like the taste of mashed potatoes
With gravy on the side.
French fries, too, will always do
As long as they've been fried.

The smell of grilled cheese sandwiches
And a pile of potato chips,
Cause me to uncontrollably
Lick my fingertips.

And hot and sugary doughnuts
Are a favorite treat of mine.
I can gobble down seven or eight,
And sometimes eight or nine.

I can take some chocolate cake
Or tasty gingerbread,
But sometimes I prefer a simple
Chili dog instead.

And breadsticks and lasagna—
That's the only way to go.
That's the lowdown in a nutshell,
And that's all there is to know.

That's my list of items
Composed of tasty treats,
But I'd rather have a root canal
Than eat a bowl of beets.

GEE WHIZ, WHAT DID WE EVER DO TO HIM?

Total Solar Eclipse

Well within our solar system,
But still in outer space,
The moon is circling around us
At an astronomical pace.

It's heading back to get in line
For a phenomenal event—
A supernatural happening
That no one can prevent.

And here we sit on planet Earth
On a straight and steady course,
To align ourselves with the sun and moon
By gravitational force.

The last time we had a total eclipse,
It quickly came and went.
It was the Earth and sun and moon in rhythm
That caused this rare event.

I saw the light around me fade
Amid a sunny afternoon,
Plunging into total darkness
By the shadow of the moon.

The Earth and moon in a constant struggle
To align with one another.
Zipping around in outer space,
And looking for each other.

Spinning here, revolving there,
And orbiting along,
Steadily whirling, twisting, and twirling
To be where they belong.

Meanwhile, the sun holds steady,
Waiting for us to align—
And, as far as I can tell,
By incredible design.

When we all line up together,
And we look up to the sky,
We see coronal filaments
As the moon goes passing by.

All this happens in an instant,
As we jockey for position.
Three celestial bodies unite
To put on this exhibition.

But the sun sits still and doesn't flinch,
Like the sun has always done.
It never has to budge an inch,
It doesn't have to—it's the sun.

Instant Butterfly

Joseph, only three years old—
A handful to be sure—
Not the least bit cultivated,
And naturally immature.

Sitting at the kitchen table
With a bib around his neck—
About to throw a temper tantrum
And make the place a wreck.

First, he took his chocolate milk
And poured it on the floor.
I guess he figured out
He didn't want it anymore.

His fork was meant to hold
The food for him to swallow.
He flung it somewhere, uncontrolled,
His spoon was soon to follow.

It was Joseph's chicken sandwich
That was next upon the list,
And like a giant monster,
He squashed it in his fist.

Then he grabbed an ear of corn
And threw it over there.
He took his mashed potatoes,
And rubbed them in his hair.

He filled his cheeks with macaroni,
And like a fire hose,
He sprayed it like a fireman
Over everybody's clothes.

He turned his fist into a hammer
And flattened his pumpkin pie,
The boy was told he shouldn't do it,
But he did not comply.

And not to be outdone
By what he'd done already,
Joseph hurled his pork-and-beans
Consistently and steady.

Next, he snatched a muffin,
And launched it toward the cat.
Then he turned his empty plate
Into a frisbee after that.

He spied a stick of butter
On the corner of his tray.
His mother shouted, "No you don't!"
His dad jumped out of the way.

And without the slightest hesitation,
With his parents standing by,
A single stick of butter
Became an instant butterfly.

It splattered on the wall
Where butter doesn't belong.
You'll notice the food on Joseph's tray
Doesn't last for very long.

By the Same Token

I play the pitchfork fluently,
It's meant for me to strum.
I pluck the tines with my fingers,
And thump it with my thumb.

The pitchfork provides the perfect pitch.
It enhances any key.
It accentuates the viola
When it plays along with me.

It's the most melodic pitchfork
Of any pitchfork ever made.
It shows those crazy clarinets
How an instrument should be played.

It's wonderful to listen to
When the oboe plays along.
The instruments blend so well together
On any given song.

It improves the sound of violins
Made by Stradivari,
And makes them sound phenomenal,
Though some opinions vary.

When it comes to making music,
I use a pitchfork when I play.
By the same token, I use the cello
When it comes to pitching hay.

Shapes

We all come in different shapes—
One no better than the other.
Most of us look like one thing,
But want to look like another.

Do not be too concerned
By your body's natural shape.
So what if you look like a raisin,
And I resemble a grape?!

You're allowed to look like a tuba,
Or an oboe if you prefer.
My teacher looks like a trumpet,
And that's okay with her.

If you're shaped like a circle,
You shouldn't become annoyed.
My brother looks like a building
That resembles a trapezoid.

My neighbor looks like a pumpkin.
Her grandmother looks like a pear,
And her cousin on her father's side
Looks exactly like a square.

My sister is shaped like a barrel,
And my nephew like a flag.
My uncle is shaped like a two-by-four,
But he doesn't like to brag.

Our mailman has the honor
Of resembling a bottle of wine.
Even if he looked like a milk jug,
He'd be perfectly fine.

Maybe you're shaped like a jukebox,
Or perhaps you look like a shoe.
Whatever you end up looking like,
You might as well look like you.

Whichever shape that you decide
Is the shape that you should be.
Let your preference be your guide,
And that'll be fine with me.

For the Most Part

Molly Mae decided one day
To open the barnyard door
And ride into town on her unicorn,
Like she hadn't done before.

Molly Mae and her unicorn
Formed the perfect pair:
The unicorn with her magic horn
And Molly's golden hair.

They walked for twenty miles
On the long and winding road,
Far enough, until they reached
A different area code.

The befuddled people stared at them
From the local general store.
They'd never seen anyone riding
On a unicorn before.

But the people there weren't buying it,
Being suspicious in their ways.
They knew unicorns didn't exist,
For the most part, nowadays.

I guess nobody told Molly Mae
This information before,
That there really is no such thing
As unicorns anymore.

Molly would probably go bananas,
And what an interesting twist
If she found out she was actually riding
A unicorn that doesn't exist.

UNICORN
HORNS
CHEAP!!!

A Time of Wonder

Long ago when time was young
And history wasn't born,
Long before the time of battles,
Before a country torn.

Before the times of feuding,
And the days of discontent,
There stood a time of wonder
That somehow came and went.

A tranquil time of splendor,
When every afternoon
Would spill into a night of dreams,
Assisted by the moon.

Where no one needed money,
No one cared about your worth,
And wealth and greed and want and need
Did not corrupt the Earth.

And every traveled road,
Stood a friend at every turn,
And the curse of ill intention
Was none of their concern.

But then without a warning,
The thing they never feared:
The time of wonder they knew so well
Somehow disappeared.

It vanished from before them,
And the only thing to learn
Was that the time of wonder
Was never to return.

Yet, no one now
Can tell me how,
And no one really knows,
Exactly how the time of wonder
Finally came to close.

But gone it has, not to return,
This departed time of wonder.
It ended quite abruptly
In a catastrophic blunder.

And the people knew
Not what to do
Nor even who to blame,
But soon they came to realize
Things would never be the same.

And unrest became a way of life,
So everybody fought.
They believed it ended arguments,
So everybody thought.

And corruption plagued authority
From the Congress to the Senate.
They swindled from the vast reserves,
And everything there in it.

And the leaders often cheated,
And the cheaters often lied,
And the people feared authority
Throughout the countryside.

And they lost the will
To reverse the curse,
So it all remains the same.
Now the people fault themselves,
For there's no one else to blame.

Time was young once long ago
When history wasn't born,
Long before the time of battles,
Before a country torn.

There stood a time of wonder,
But to everyone's surprise,
The brawling and the bickering
Led to its demise.

A Bona Fide Education

I never took a single exam,
And I didn't study science.
I didn't keep up with current events,
I relied on self-reliance.

I never examined arithmetic.
Calculus wasn't my focus.
And I always thought of trigonometry
As some bogus hocus-pocus.

I never tackled astronomy
Or gravitational force,
Though I signed up for astrophysics,
I never took the course.

I showed no interest in writing—
It's obvious, as you can tell.
I always use words that are simple to read,
And not too hard to spell.

I never had a history lesson,
Not one that I can recall.
Nor did I crack a single book,
Or take any notes at all.

Schoolwork was always something
That I never had to do,
For these are mostly subject matters
That I already knew.

I have no legal certification
Or prestigious PhD.
Who needs a bona fide education
When you're as smart as me?

The Medicine Man

There's an illness infecting
The tribal nation,
Which calls for some expert
Evaluation.

So the Medicine Man
Is summoned to see
If he knows the solution
And what it could be.

He concocts a potion
Of carnelian stones
And the sacred remains
Of some animal bones.

Ritually clad
In ceremonious attire,
He mixes ingredients
Over the fire.

He embarks in the dark
By the light of the moon,
After pondering the issues
All afternoon.

He calls on the spirits
Of the Blackfoot Tribe
To harness their energy
And ethereal vibe.

Fanning the fumes
That fill the air
While a night owl watches
The whole affair.

Gazing at stars
He chants an ancient tongue
That he learned from his elders
When he was young.

Flying embers
From the crackling flame
Fall back to Earth
From where they came.

The burning inferno
Warms the night,
While shadows shiver
In the flickering light.

He summons the wisdom
From ancestral graves
For the unknown remedy
He desperately craves.

He isn't a doctor.
He's not a physician.
He holds no credentials
In his current position.

It's a shot in the dark,
But with so much at stake,
This is a shot
That he's willing to take.

And no one actually
Knows for sure
If the Medicine Man
Can find a cure.

But nobody heals
Like the Medicine Man
And if he can't do it,
Nobody can.

An Ingenious Contraption

What's that contraption
Making that sound?
Lo and behold,
It's a merry-go-round!

It's spinning in place,
It's revolving around,
It's coming to life—
With a jubilant sound.

The bangs are banging.
The dings are dinging.
The clangs are clanging,
And the bells are ringing.

The whistles are whistling.
The gears are grinding.
The colors are glistening,
And the lights are blinding.

There's a crowd in line
To climb onboard,
For a three-minute ride
That can't be ignored.

They're unconcerned
With anything more.
They're having more fun
Than they were having before.

So many attractions
You can ride at the fair,
But the great carousel
Is the champion there.

So I'm climbing aboard
And spending the day,
Spinning my primary
Troubles away.

On a whirling machine
With a mechanical chorus—
What an ingenious contraption
We have before us!

I Almost Forgot

Danger is all around me
As I creep along the ground,
Right through a den of sleeping lions
That I wish I'd never found.

I happened upon them accidentally,
And there's only one thing to do:
Tiptoe by them undetected
And hope I make it through.

I dare not wake the sleeping cats,
For they'll be quick to strike.
Then I'd be in a predicament
That I really wouldn't like.

Now, if I continue nice and quiet,
Maybe I'll survive
And live to tell this amazing story,
If I make it out alive.

In these uncertain situations
There are no guarantees—
And I almost forgot, I'm allergic to cats,
And I really have to sneeze!

Conduct Unbecoming

When I think of elementary school,
I remember very well
Standing in the corner
And waiting for the bell.

It's all because I overlooked
The rules they put in place.
So there I stood with those two walls,
Inches from my face.

I used to sneak into forbidden places
Where the other students wouldn't,
But then I got in trouble
For being where I shouldn't.

I seemed to cause disorder
By running down the hall.
So there I stood in the corner
Facing toward the wall.

And right there in the corner,
Like so many times before,
I waited nearly motionless
For hours, maybe more.

Mrs. Turner didn't want me
Ignoring regulations.
I disrupted the class
And her daily operations.

So she stood me in the corner
For those offensive actions,
And for conduct unbecoming,
And my overall infractions.

But my teacher didn't realize
From her authoritative position,
That this was where my imagination
Came into fruition.

Thoughts of being someone
Like an international spy,
Or pretending I'm a hummingbird
Zipping through the sky.

Or sometimes I impersonated
The mighty Captain Hook,
Or maybe I was Silverstein
Writing another book.

And there were times when daydreams
Had my full attention,
And then I was Eli Whitney,
Creating some invention.

Whatever were the circumstances,
The corner proved to be
The ideal spot for imagination
For a visionary like me.

All this happened years ago
But I can still recall,
That standing in the corner
Never bothered me at all.

Ten-Foot Pole

There lives a goat,
But not in a zoo,
Who eats all day,
But not like you.

He lives in a junkyard
Feeding on scraps,
Food that would make
Your stomach collapse.

He chows down on motors
From a broken-down racer,
Then swallows some rotors
With an antifreeze chaser.

He gnaws upon batteries
For a midnight snack,
And chases it down
With a hydraulic jack.

He'll gorge on a toolbox
Like a demon possessed,
First goes the hammer,
Then goes the rest.

He burps when he crunches.
He grunts when he chews.
He'll swallow your socks
While he's eating your shoes.

He spends half the morning
On wrought iron pans,
And finishes the day
By chewing on cans.

He'll feast upon glass,
The fragments ingested,
Then lies in the grass
While the shards are digested.

But mostly he loves
To chew on your hat,
And gorge on your gloves,
And right after that—

He'll snack upon sawdust,
There's no need for butter.
He'll gobble up golf clubs
Right down to the putter.

He'll pig out on tires
From bicycles, and then,
Tune in tomorrow,
And he'll do it again.

You don't have to boil it,
Or fry it, or heat it,
If it's something worth eating,
Believe me, he'll eat it.

But fix him a pot roast
With potatoes and roll,
And he wouldn't touch it
With a ten-foot pole!

The Rocking Chair Brothers

A couple of brothers long ago
Were wondering what to do.
So together they built some rocking chairs,
Simple, strong, and true.

Cutting and carving the pieces of wood
Was done by the older brother.
The shaping, forming, and fitting and such
Was completed by the other.

They crafted so many rocking chairs,
They eventually opened a store.
To sell the chairs to people who wanted
One, or two, or more.

But the chairs grew dusty,
And the brothers old,
Wondering in frustration,
Why never a chair had ever been sold—
Neither had an explanation.

Henry's Job

Henry takes the magazines,
And walks around and sells them.
Because Henry's boss gives the orders,
So Henry does what he tells him.

And if Henry doesn't follow orders,
His boss gets mad and yells them.
So Henry takes the magazines,
And walks around and sells them.

Penguins and Ostriches

Penguins and ostriches do not fly,
But I'm a little bit confused.
They both have me wondering why
They have wings they've never used.

They have two wings that they can flap,
And they walk like birds should walk.
They have feathers that overlap,
And they talk like birds should talk.

They fit the profile of normal birds,
Having identical features.
Everything about them says to me,
These are similar creatures.

The penguin sits and wonders
How the ostrich takes the heat.
The ostrich questions how the penguin
Deals with ice beneath his feet.

They should fly like pelicans
Or eagles, hawks, and crows.
So why they remain on solid ground
Nobody really knows.

Perhaps they're simply stubborn
In their own rebellious ways.
They don't even fly around
On special holidays.

Penguins and ostriches do not fly,
Yet have wings on either side.
Maybe they haven't learned to flap,
Or perhaps they've never tried.

Neither one has flown at all
And I think I've figured out why.
These two must be scared of heights
Otherwise, they would fly.

Dad's Dozer

My dad drives a dozer
To work every day,
And pushes the traffic
Out of his way.

Teenagers avoid him,
So they can survive.
Old men insult him,
Yelling, "Learn how to drive!"

Grandmothers scold him
Throughout the day.
With their heads out the window,
Screaming, "Get out of the way!"

He creates hostilities,
But it doesn't make him quit.
It never seems to bother
My father a bit.

He keeps pushing the traffic
Out of his way,
By driving his dozer
To work every day.

Magicians

I drew a card from the deck,
Then slid it back inside.
The magician found the card I chose.
I stood there mystified.

Then he produced a puff of smoke
From nothing but the air,
Repeated some magic words,
And changed an apple to a pear.

He casually dropped a handkerchief
That floated to the floor.
He waved his magic wand
To produce a dozen more.

He made a quarter disappear.
And right before my eyes,
Made a nickel reappear—
All to my surprise.

Created fire out of nowhere,
Pulled a rabbit from a hat,
Split a woman in two pieces—
What could go wrong with that?

He switched an ordinary rubber ball
From a circle to a square,
And caught a bullet with his teeth—
What could go wrong there?

Spectators first had their misgivings,
But now they all believe.
There's no telling how many gimmicks
This guy had up his sleeve.

He performed a hundred tricks
And some mind-blowing illusions,
Leaving the audience sitting there
To draw their own conclusions.

Magicians have a special talent
And some secrets to conceal.
It's incredible how magicians
Make the impossible seem real.

Seven Words a Minute

She's been typing for forty years,
Now her fingers are tired.
Her thumb is numb, so it appears,
And it's time that she retired.

Seven words a minute she types.
That's what she's up to now.
Nobody knows how she types that fast,
But she types that fast somehow.

They'd rather keep her working there,
That's what they'd prefer.
Because no one could replace someone
Who types as fast as her.

A Little Competition

I'm too tall for basketball,
More competitive than a jockey.
I like scoring goals on ice,
But I'm too mean for hockey.

I'm too laid back for baseball,
Too relaxed for that sort of thing.
I'm too tough for football,
Too strong for the boxing ring.

I'm too quick for track and field.
I outperform everyone in it.
I'm too reckless to ride a bull,
Even for half a minute.

Way too accurate for bowling;
Too disciplined for darts;
Much too dangerous for karate
And the other martial arts.

I'm like a shark in water,
Or a gorilla lifting weights.
I'm like a knight at jousting,
And a pro on roller skates.

No one can match my fitness level,
So I have no opposition.
All I'm looking for in this world,
Is a little competition.

Doesn't matter which event I'm in,
I'm always in command,
But I can't beat a five-year-old,
Even once at Candyland.

My Ophthalmologist

My eyesight was surely failing,
Getting much too hard to see,
So I asked my ophthalmologist
What he thought was wrong with me.

He told me that for certain
It's glasses I will need,
And I would need to wear them
When I blink and look and read.

He said that I should wear them
If I ever read a book.
He said that I should use them
When I read and blink and look.

"Wear them for a week or so
When you look and read and blink,
Then come back and tell me
Exactly what you think."

So I fastened glasses to my face
With a giant rubber band,
Like the doctor told me to,
If I'm to understand.

I wore them for about a week,
Like he suggested I should do.
He told me that would do the trick,
And clear my cloudy view.

But seven days have come and gone,
And it's harder now to see.
It's amazing how mistaken
My ophthalmologist can be.

My Greatest Dilemma

Underneath the big top,
Between the circus lights,
Up here on the tightrope,
At death-defying heights,

I'm balanced on a narrow cable
A hundred feet in the air.
Daredevils want to do what I do,
But not too many dare.

The capacity crowd below me
Has seen it all before.
They're waiting for me to slip and fall,
And tumble to the floor.

So step by step, I make my way
Across the narrow wire.
A wobble or two under my shoe,
And I'm glad I'm not any higher.

And there's no net to catch me,
Should I begin to fall,
No rescue team to fetch me—
I have no help at all.

I'm high upon a narrow cable,
And there's danger down below,
But that's minor compared
To my greatest dilemma:
I've got to scratch my toe.

Who Are We to Question?

Why did the chicken cross the road?
What could be the reason?
It could be that time of year:
Chicken-road-crossing season.

Chickens throughout history
Have crossed a lot of roads,
Exactly like their counterparts—
The opossums and the toads.

They don't even check for traffic.
They don't have a clue.
They simply want to cross the road,
Because that's what chickens do.

Oh, to reach the opposite side
Where all good chickens venture,
Sometimes a chicken simply needs
A little more adventure.

They think that life is better
There, on the other side.
And chickens often try their luck
At something they've never tried.

So after gathering up the nerve
And looking at their feet,
They precisely and meticulously
Make their way across the street.

If crossing the busy highway
Is what a chicken prefers,
Then who are we to question
When all of this occurs?

They want to be on the other side
That's the reason that they go,
But why they want to be there?
Perhaps we'll never know.

Maybe the most obvious reason
Is the reason we can't ignore.
Maybe chickens just like to be
Where they've never been before.

Benji and Benny

Benji and Benny
Were eating their lunch—
Benny, a little
Benji, a bunch.

Benny was picky
With the food on his platter.
Benji was not,
So it didn't matter.

Benji's now eating
What Benny did not,
Because Benji can eat
Even more than a lot.

Benji likes anything
You put on his plate,
And eats in a hurry—
Benny can wait.

Benji likes food
Either chilly or hot,
Because Benji likes eating,
Benny does not.

Benny is skinny
From noggin to knee.
Benji is bigger
Than Benji should be.

Benji and Benny
Are the best of friends,
But that's where the only
Coincidence ends.

These are the variations
Between Benji and Benny,
Similarities, few,
The differences, many.

Let That Sink In (Howard's Idea)

The kitchen sink knocked
On the old front door—
A door that the sink
Had not seen before.

It was only a sink
For the kitchen, you see,
That was trying to get
Where it needed to be.

The door stayed defiant,
And would not let him in.
For the door didn't know
Where that sink had been.

"You may not enter!"
The front door insisted,
But the sink knocked again,
And it persisted.

This battle went on
For hours and hours,
As no truce transpired
Between the two powers.

But it came to fruition
Quite suddenly, when,
The dirty dishes cried out,
"Let that sink in!"

Snooze Button

There I was, fast asleep,
When suddenly I awoke.
I thought that I was dreaming,
And I thought it was a joke.

Because I was in a peaceful slumber
Well beyond relaxation,
When all at once my alarm clock
Changed the situation.

I hit the snooze button automatically,
Fell back asleep and then,
Not five minutes later
The clock rang out again.

Then I began my old routine,
Which is always exactly the same.
When quickly I came to realize
The snooze button was to blame.

Why am I using the snooze button
When it causes so much stress?
I never want to use the thing,
But I use it nonetheless.

It seems somebody had the crazy idea
That the alarm clock should be updated,
And so the stupid snooze button
Was eventually created.

And whoever invented the useless thing
Should be run clean out of town.
It's what the public really wants
When you really break it down.

And, honestly, I can say
I've been annoyed by this invention
One too many times today,
And more than I care to mention.

But everybody uses one
Though no one really cares to.
We should boycott that ridiculous button,
But no one ever dares to.

I know I'm guilty of oversleeping
Every once in a while,
But I can't wait for the snooze button
To finally go out of style.

Point and Giggle and Laugh

I bang my head on the ceiling.
I stumble over the chair.
I've got this terrible feeling
That my head's too high in the air.

I duck when I walk into a room.
I dodge the chandelier.
I stoop to avoid the ceiling fan
Whenever one is near.

I tread right over the picket fence.
I sidestep around the trees.
I avoid the lowest branches,
So I don't shatter my knees.

I scrape my scalp on the shingles.
I singe my hair on the light.
My ears poke into a dusty attic
Nearly every single night.

I can peek through a four-story window
While standing flat on the ground,
And I don't have to stretch my neck
Just to have a look around.

There's no one to talk to way up here.
No one can hear what I say,
So two-way conversations are minimal
On any given day.

People can't help but stop and stare,
For I stand incredibly high.
I can see almost anywhere,
And I don't have to try.

It's common for the public, I suppose,
To point and giggle and laugh,
But everyone knows, that's how it goes
If you happen to be a giraffe.

Introducing Legislation

It's against the law to steal anything
Or sell merchandise that's hot.
If you ever get caught violating these laws,
You'll be arrested on the spot.

There are laws in place against looting.
And it's against the law to riot
And making noise in the library
When you really should be quiet.

There's a law in place against arson,
And there are laws against assault.
They'll lock you up immediately
If it turns out to be your fault.

But even with all the laws on the books
There's another law we need.
It's a law that we should pass at once
With supersonic speed.

So file the necessary paperwork,
And commence with its creation.
Because if there isn't a law against foolishness,
We should introduce the legislation.

Monday Seems to Be the Day

Of all the seven days we have
To deal with every week,
There's one day in particular
That's incredibly unique.

It's a day that we're familiar with,
In this one particular case,
That seems to be the most oppressive
To the human race.

It's a day I often wonder
If it's a day we even need.
It's a day of little value—
A useless day indeed.

Monday is the day, I say,
It's the day, without a doubt.
It's the only one of seven days
That we can do without.

Monday is the day, I say,
That everybody hates.
No day provokes animosity
As much as Monday generates.

Monday is the day, I say,
I think we all agree.
Monday is the only day
That should never ever be.

Six would be enough for us
In the world we live today.
So Monday is the only day
We need to throw away.

Monday is the day that is
Despised from coast to coast.
Monday seems to be the day
We love to hate the most.

My Report Card

My report card isn't flattering,
If the truth be told.
It's nothing to admire,
And it's nothing to behold.

If you saw my report card,
You would not believe it.
I should throw it in the trash can,
And turn around and leave it.

Or toss it in the shredder,
Or light the thing on fire,
Or wash it in the washer,
And mangle it in the dryer.

Or I could locate a magician,
Who would gladly interfere
And find some clever way
To make it disappear.

There must be some technique
To somehow rearrange it,
Or perhaps my teacher would see fit
And allow me to exchange it.

The other students in my class
Should all consider trading,
For they have great report cards
With nearly perfect grading.

My report card isn't flattering,
That's the bottom line.
If I could only find someone
To swap their card with mine.

Punching Bag

My brother has a strange obsession,
And this is how I know:
He uses me for a punching bag
For every single blow.

It seems he has the notion
And the obvious impression
That I'm his personal punching bag
To use at his discretion.

It's all because it's so convenient,
As anyone can see.
He doesn't own a punching bag,
So my brother punches me.

From the moment I awaken,
Until I go to bed,
He doesn't use a punching bag—
He uses me instead.

His punches hurt my arm so much
That I've become paranoid,
And his punches are exactly
What I am trying to avoid.

So I've begun a new campaign
To bring about awareness,
For this is such a worthy cause,
And it's all about the fairness.

I have to raise some money,
Because equipment isn't free,
To purchase him a punching bag
As quickly as can be.

Then hang it from the rafters
Or suspend it from a tree,
Then he can use the punching bag,
Instead of using me.

Mr. Kazoo

Mr. Kazoo
Was tying his shoe,
Because that's all he ever
Knew how to do.

He couldn't type.
He couldn't cook.
He couldn't read
Any words in a book.

He couldn't fix
A simple machine.
He couldn't peel
A tangerine.

He couldn't dance.
He couldn't sing.
That Mr. Kazoo
Couldn't do a thing!

Except when it came
To tying his shoe,
He didn't know much,
But that much he knew.

Make up Your Mind

It's too hot for you to sleep tonight—
It's too hot to stay awake.
But you must do either one of the two—
It's a tough decision to make.

You perspire in your clothing,
No matter what you wear.
I'll even bet you break out in a sweat
Every time you comb your hair.

You're panting when you brush your teeth
Behind the bathroom door
And you can't seem to ever manage
To cool off anymore.

It's too hot to ride in the motorboat.
It's too hot to mow the lawn.
It's too hot to handle the TV remote
To turn the television on!

You don't ride your bicycle
Because your butt sticks to the seat.
And you don't help in the kitchen
Because you can't stand the heat.

You insisted that we move away
To where it's not so hot.
You were anxious for a change
But, quite honestly, I was not.

So we moved up to the Arctic Circle
Because I was always told,
That, frankly, you couldn't stand the heat,
And now you deplore the cold.

Booby Trap

I raced the fastest kid in school.
He beat me just like that.
He ran around the soccer field
In forty seconds flat.

Then we raced across the schoolyard
So he really poured it on
I had only started running—
When I looked, and he was gone.

Then we tried it once again,
And I was curious to see
If I was even going to win
At least one out of three.

As usual, he was way ahead
On the third and final run,
But then I sprang my booby trap
And, miraculously, I won.

Day Job

If you want to go to the ball game,
I'm telling you in advance,
You'll be busy otherwise,
And you won't get the chance.

If you want to spend the whole day
Lounging at the beach,
Let me make it obvious,
It's far beyond your reach.

Play some golf on your vacation?
This is only a mirage.
There's no time for recreation—
Leave the clubs in your garage.

There's a concert at the forum,
But I'm here to let you know,
You can just forget about it,
You won't have time to go.

Want tickets to the colosseum
For the undisputed fight?
You don't have the option,
You won't be there tonight.

Instead, you'll have to spend your time
In an all familiar scene.
Growing weary in your overall,
Ridiculous routine.

No chance to go where you want to go,
Only to do as you're told.
Your day job seems to make it so,
And it's getting rather old.

The situation you're facing now
Is really nothing new.
Working hampers the process
Of everything you do.

You'd rather do what you want to do
Each and every day,
But ever notice how your day job
Always gets in the way?

Blaze a Trail

Travel time is not a care,

Because I'm never in a hurry.

From anywhere

To over there,

I'm never one to scurry.

You won't see me pick up steam

Even when I'm late.

It's a constant delay

When I slither away

At this apathetic rate.

It's not that I'm lazy or loafing around,
That would be false, indeed.
I keep in stride
And always decide
My very own rate of speed.

No matter where I'm coming from,
No matter where I go,
In either case
I keep the pace
And take it nice and slow.

I don't advise one imitating
My lackadaisical style.
I always say
From far away,
"I'll be along in a while."

There's no acceleration
In my current situation,
And I don't blaze a trail.
I creep and I crawl because, after all,
That's life when you're a snail.

That's When It All Went Crazy

You can imagine my dilemma,
And how hungry I had to be
To hire a local lumberjack
To fix a BLT.

All I wanted was a sandwich for lunch,
But a chef could not be found.
I looked throughout the entire kitchen,
But there were none around.

So I hired a local lumberjack—
What else could I do?
Someone had to fix my sandwich
And slice the thing in two.

He prepared a BLT
As dandy as a daisy,
But when it came time to cut the thing,
That's when it all went crazy.

He lifted his mighty axe to the sky
And with one ferocious swing,
Disembodied my BLT
And disintegrated the thing.

The bacon was completely mangled,
The lettuce became contorted.
The bread was simply pulverized,
And the tomato was distorted.

I tried to piece it back together,
But I would soon discover
That there was nothing left to use
And nothing to recover.

Lumberjacks are good with lumber
When it's time to chop a tree,
But not at cutting sandwiches,
As you can plainly see.

Big Hairy Monsters

Monsters big and hairy
Are very, very scary.
They're not a friendly species,
And this is legendary.

So you must be diligent
And extra cautionary
When dealing with this typical,
And formidable adversary.

You'll need to hire a security guard,
Or at least a secretary,
To be always on the lookout
For monsters big and hairy.

But at times they're unavoidable
And you'll find it necessary
To cross the street or reconfigure
Your whole itinerary.

For they'll confront you constantly—
That's not out of the ordinary.
So continue looking over your shoulder
For monsters big and hairy.

Because big and hairy monsters
Are not imaginary,
And you can find the proof
In any dictionary.

It's best to be a little leery
And a bit precautionary
When encountering hairy monsters—
It's only customary.

So be cautious and be wary
Of monsters big and hairy.
For they are really scary.
Yes, they can be, very.

Must I Brush My Teeth Again?

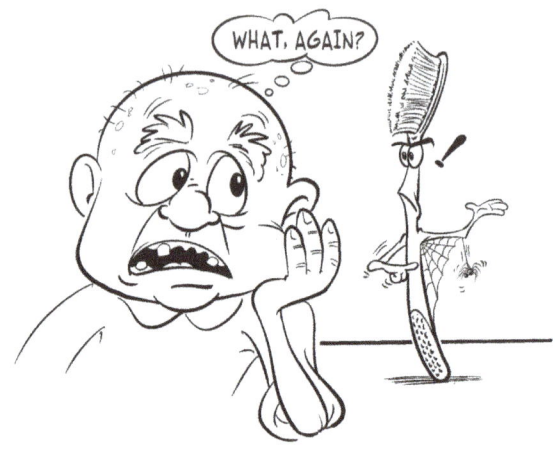

I've got thousands of toothbrushes
And gallons of Listerine.
My pile of oral hygiene products
Beats all you've ever seen.

I have enough fluoride toothpaste
To fill up the Suez Canal,
And more than enough dental floss
To fence off the O.K. Corral.

I have no need for X-rays
Or prescriptions I must fill.
I've never purchased dentures,
And I doubt I ever will.

However, my dentist has informed me,
By way of certified letter,
That I should brush my teeth again—
And the sooner I do, the better.

But I don't want to brush my teeth anymore,
So I will graciously decline.
Besides, I already brushed my teeth
Back in 1979!

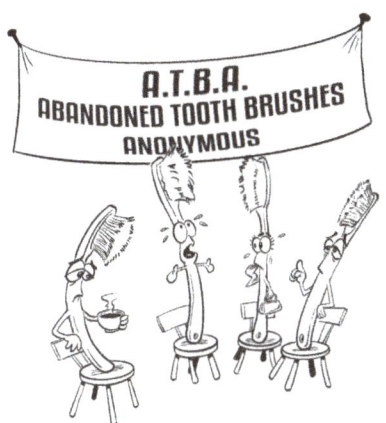

As Far as the Eye Can See

It's time to paint the sky above—
It's long been overdue—
A vibrant tint
With the slightest hint
Of psychedelic blue.

And I'm the one to do the job,
So leave it all to me.
I'll paint the skies
Before your eyes
As blue as blue can be.

By the time I'm finished painting
You won't believe your eyes,
I guarantee
That you will see
Perfection in the skies.

I have all the supplies required,
I've got the whole procedure planned.
I've got a thousand buckets
Of the bluest paint
And a paintbrush in my hand.

I've set up all the scaffolding
To reach up to the sky.
The ladder's in place,
And just in case,
There's an ambulance standing by.

I'm completely motivated
And now I'm ready to do it,
But I've discovered someone else
Has already beat me to it.

It seems a painter long ago
Had the same idea as me,
And already painted the entire sky
As far as the eye can see.

Now I need to understand
Exactly what I'm to do
With this brush I'm holding in my hand
And all this extra blue.

I should've considered my surroundings
And showed some self-restraint,
And maybe I should've looked up first,
Before I bought the paint.

A Toe Like You

You're the best poet
As some poets go,
But how you do it,
I wouldn't know.

Whatever the place,
Whenever the time,
You seem to know
About composing a rhyme.

You put words in order,
So perfectly placed—
Efficiently choreographed
And evenly spaced.

You make it look easy,
You make it complete.
I tried to do it,
But I couldn't compete.

I have no talent,
That much I know.
You have more genius
In your little toe.

So I sit here and dream
Of the things I could do.
If only I had
A toe like you.

All These Keys

I heard the distinctive sound
Of a piano in my ear,
Like someone had succeeded
In their musical career.

I thought it would be phenomenal
If I too could learn to play,
With instructions or without them—
I'd try it either way.

I wouldn't mind the lessons
If I have the supplies I need,
Like a piano right in front of me
And some music here to read.

Now sit me down and move aside,
I'm gonna learn to play.
Even though I've never tried,
I suggest you clear the way.

I don't need to harmonize,
And I don't need to sing,
Just give me a snazzy piano,
And let me do my thing!

Let's get the best that money can buy—
A Steinway would be nice—
The quality is comparable
And related to the price.

Place it in the music room,
If space in there will allow.
If there wasn't one in there before,
There'll certainly be one now.

I must simply take the incentive,
And realize my fate.
The world awaits my expertise,
And I won't make them wait.

Now the piano is in front of me,
And the stool is on the floor,
I just need to figure out
What all these keys are for!

The World's Fastest Barber

BEFORE   AFTER

I WONDER WHEN HE'S GONNA START?

If you go to see the barber
On the busy side of town,
He will surely cut your hair
As soon as you sit down.

He's the fastest barber
When it comes to cutting hair.
It only takes him fifteen seconds
While you're sitting there.

He'll proceed with blinding speed
Scissors busy snipping.
Satisfaction guaranteed—
Clippers busy clipping.

And when he's through with cutting you,
And your hair is on the floor,
You'll still look the same, it's true,
Only different than before.

He cuts hair for anyone
Ages five to ninety-nine,
And with no mistakes,
Then he takes whoever's next in line.

He'll cut yours and he'll cut mine,
But everyone beware—
It takes three hours of waiting in line
Just to get into the chair.

In the Middle of the Day

I was simply sitting there
In the middle of the day,
Looking for a way to chase
These hunger blues away.

And so to cure this craving
I looked for something to eat—
Something that was simple,
Something sort of sweet.

Something not too hard to make
That's easy to prepare.
I looked around, and then I found
An apple sitting there.

The only apple I could see,
Fat and juicy for the taking,
As red as any apple could be,
There was no mistaking.

But when I peeled this apple,
I broke into a sweat.
My shirt became quite saturated
And my face was soaking wet.

Then there came a sudden chill
Up and down my spine,
And everything went haywire
Right on down the line.

I went into convulsions,
And I started flipping out,
And I began to understand
What peeling apples was about.

The burden was more than I could bear,
My nerves were out of whack.
It took longer than I thought it would,
Just to get my rhythm back.

The physical strain was an enormous drain,
I was weary from the drama.
And it took another twenty-four hours
To recover from the trauma.

Apples are the perfect snack—
They're absolutely ideal—
But I never knew that apples
Were so difficult to peel.

If I ever peel another apple,
I'll find another way.
I'm not used to exerting that much energy
In the middle of the day.

Life Was So Much Easier

She's the oldest person there is,
And her birthday is today.
She's had a lot of birthdays before,
And more are on the way.

At a hundred and ninety-nine years old,
I can almost guarantee
That she can hardly hear a thing,
And she can barely see.

She won't let that bother her now—
It's a day for celebration.
But we're having a little trouble
With the birthday cake situation.

The baker said, "This cake will handle
All the candles you can fit!"
So I just lit every birthday candle
That was ever supposed to be lit.

Who knows in a year from now
Where the candles will be placed?
Two hundred candles will have to work,
Or the celebration's gone to waste.

We'll either have to do one of two things,
So as not to make a mistake:
Either we'll have to use smaller candles,
Or she'll need a bigger cake.

And two hundred candles a year from now
Is reason to celebrate,
But life was so much easier
When she was only a hundred and ninety-eight.

The Dirtiest Place on Earth

I stay dirty all the time—
I'm not squeaky clean.
I'm not exactly sanitary
In my everyday routine.

I never need to take a bath
Or ever wash my hair.
I never have to take a shower,
And I don't really care.

I don't mind my messy face,
And I'm not spick and span.
I live in the dirtiest place on Earth
And stay as filthy as I can.

My clothes are never ironed.
My house is never clean.
It's like this seven days a week
And every day between.

You'll not see me use a broom,
And I don't need a mop.
It's the way I choose to live,
And I will never stop.

First I wiggle, then I wobble,
I squiggle and I squirm.
I crawl around,
Deep underground—
I like that I'm a worm.

Think About It

When you buy new transportation,
Something practical will do,
Where basic elements are plentiful,
And amenities are few.

Something good on gasoline—
That would be the goal.
Something simple to handle
And easy to control,

That wouldn't draw much attention
When you get behind the wheel,
That's not a bit spectacular,
And not that big a deal.

After surveying everything out there,
Now it's time to climb aboard.
It's only ninety million dollars,
So it's easy to afford.

You've decided on a mega yacht—
The practical way to go.
It has five decks above it,
And several down below.

It's two hundred feet from bow to stern,
And sleeps a dozen guests.
It fulfills maritime requirements
And passes all the tests.

First, you find a place to dock it,
Then you hire the crew,
Get the proper permits signed,
And that's all you have to do.

But there is maintenance on the vessel
And taxes you must pay,
Harbor expenses and docking fees
All along the way.

There is much to consider here—
You'd better think about it a lot.
Think about it before you buy
A ninety million-dollar yacht.

Isolated Whereabouts

Entwined between the mountains
And the waves that break the shore,
Beneath the cloudy canopy,
Beyond the desert floor,

Lies a land of simple splendor
That no one's ever known,
For no one's ever had the chance
To call the land their own.

Where the sky is always blue,
And the wind is often still,
Along the open mesa,
Beside a silent hill.

Where no one ever felled a tree,
For no one ever should,
Where feet have never trampled,
And no one ever stood.

In an area seen by no one,
Well-hidden from the eye,
A detective couldn't find it,
And neither could a spy.

Its isolated whereabouts
Will never see the day
The real estate developers
Ever get their way.

It's better than the beach,
More tranquil than seclusion.
If you think there's somewhere better,
It's only an illusion.

A region drenched in solitude,
Rarely seen today.
A location you could visit,
If you only knew the way.

Nobody lives around it,
It's undiscovered still,
For no one's ever found it,
And no one ever will.

The ocean isn't far away.
The mountain's right behind it,
And I would travel there today,
If I knew where to find it.

Jigsaw Puzzle

This jigsaw puzzle
Is hard to do,
So I'll use a hammer
Or maybe some glue.

Too many pieces
To sort it all out—
Too much to decipher
What this puzzle's about.

I've examined the pieces
Bit by bit,
I've studied them well,
But how do they fit?

Should I toil any longer
To make the connections,
Or pick up the box
And read the directions?

Do I need a professor
To help me to see?
Is that the idea—
How hard can it be?

It's scrambled to bits,
It's an organized mess.
How it all fits
Is anyone's guess.

I'm giving up now
Because I've had enough.
These two-piece puzzles
Can sure be tough.

Bamboo Fishing Poles

They've got fishing poles made of plastic now
For catching trout and bass.
They even have them if you want one
Made of fiberglass.

They have them made of carbon fiber
For fishing all day long,
And superstrength titanium,
If you want one superstrong.

They make them out of aluminum too
For featherweight operation.
So casting goes much smoother now
When you're fishing on vacation.

New fishing poles are constructed
In so many different ways.
I guess bamboo is impossible
To acquire nowadays.

Closet Space

I had to move into a closet
From where I lived before,
Because it costs too much for me
To live there anymore.

First, I slid my bed inside
Right up against the wall,
Which nearly took up all the room,
If there was any room at all.

I sorted my belongings
Into what little room remained.
Now everything is packed inside
And very well-contained.

But it's tough to do my laundry—
There's nowhere to wash my clothes—
And no place to put my TV set
To watch my favorite shows.

I'd like to hang some pictures
And display my prized possessions,
But I simply do not have the room
To exhibit self-expressions.

There is no running water,
And a shower wouldn't fit,
And not one place in this tiny space
For anyone to sit.

My ability to maneuver
Is certainly concerning.
I'm always bumping into something
No matter where I'm turning.

Extra room is hard to find,
Not much space to spare.
There's not much room that's over here,
There's not much over there.

How long I will live in here,
I don't really know.
The future isn't really clear,
But the rent is very low.

And it's easy to maintain,
I can tell you that.
I can dust the entire closet
In twenty seconds flat.

My mailbox sits outside the door,
My goldfish by the wall,
And the bathroom, when I need it,
Is only down the hall.

The unassuming area
Is free of interruptions,
So I can usually concentrate
With limited disruptions.

When you reside inside a closet,
You leave the world behind.
It's adequately tranquil,
But space is hard to find.

The Incredible Speed of Light

Onlookers take notice,
Bystanders behold,
And bear witness to this event.
If you blink an eye, it'll pass you by,
And you'll wonder where it went.

Spectators observe,
Stand up and attest,
And I will guarantee
That no one can master anything faster
Than what you're about to see.

It can exceed the fastest speed
Of anything day or night.
Not a thing, it would seem,
With a good head of steam
Can equal the speed of light.

It's quicker than rabbits
With hoppity habits,
More rapid than things can fly.
It'll beat any train
Humankind can obtain
Or spaceship that money can buy.

Not even NASA can build a contraption
That can match the incredible speed.
There's nothing out there
Flying through the air
That light cannot exceed.

It can beat the fastest feet,
It's more rapid than a glance.
And all those cars
At the Indy Five Hundred
Don't even stand a chance.

It beats any bird you've ever seen
Or any sound you've ever heard.
It's even quicker
Than the quickest machine,
So take me at my word.

It obliterates bullets lickety-split,
And comets have limited chances.
It can scat like a cat
In two seconds flat,
Regardless of circumstances.

It can surpass
And even outclass
The speediest satellite.
It's safe to say,
That, as of today,
Nothing is faster than light.

From a tumbleweed
To astronomical speed,
To the fastest meteorite—
Young and old,
Stand up and behold
The incredible speed of light.

Liquid World of Mine

I don't need a boat to sail.
I don't take the train.
I don't need the city bus,
And I don't need a plane.

I don't require mountains
To climb upon and then,
Turn around to make my way
Right back down again.

I don't roam the forest
With a hundred thousand trees.
It's somewhere else altogether
You'll find my expertise.

I swim around secure and free,
The water suits me fine.
The perfect way for me to be
In this liquid world of mine.

All I need is oxygen
And the deep blue open sea,
And where I am at anytime
Is where I need to be.

I only require unlimited room
The evidence has shown.
The space that I must utilize
Is mine and mine alone.

And I can say with certainty
From the marrow of my soul,
It's great to be a goldfish
Swimming in a bowl.

This Always Seems to Happen

This apple tastes like an apricot,
And bananas taste like berries.
Meatloaf tastes like melon,
And chocolate tastes like cherries.

My bacon tastes like lima beans,
I assume this sugar is salt.
This carrot seems like a cantaloupe,
And mushrooms just like malt.

This orange tastes like oatmeal.
This peach tastes like a pear.
The grapes I'm having taste like gravy
And a freshly baked éclair.

Tomatoes are like tangerines.
Doughnuts taste like the deli.
Tuna reminds me of tenderloin,
And jerky, a bit like jelly.

Vanilla has a vinegar tang,
Which is very strange to me,
And strawberries favor spaghetti—
That is not how it should be.

My pancakes taste like pizza.
This pineapple tastes like plum.
Lasagna's too much like licorice,
And garlic, exactly like gum.

While lemons seem like liver,
And lobster tastes like lamb,
It's a very unusual circumstance
When halibut tastes like ham.

These waffles taste like wine,
From some chateau in France.
Food should not be this confusing,
Under any circumstance.

And did I happen to mention
That sauerkraut tastes like shark?
This always seems to happen
When I'm eating in the dark.

Bananas

In downtown Savannah,
While taking a stroll,
I slipped on a banana,
And I lost control.

My balance was off.
My perception was faltered.
My stability shifted.
My judgement was altered.

I slid down the pavement,
Like a runaway train,
Knocking down bikers
In the bicycle lane.

I zigzagged once,
I spun around twice,
Like an ice skater does
When skating on ice.

I skirted by a dog,
Lying there dreaming,
And a Girl Scout troop
That ran away screaming.

I drifted by boys
On skateboards and bikes,
And a grumpy old man
That nobody likes.

I skimmed down the sidewalk
In different directions,
For thirteen blocks
And twelve intersections.

I took out a stop sign,
And on the way through,
I knocked down a dozen
Pedestrians too.

I eventually landed
Flat on my face,
After causing hysteria
All over the place.

Hundreds of people
Were dazed and confused.
The public was terrified,
Battered and bruised.

Some had contusions,
Others, abrasions,
But that's how it goes
On these perilous occasions.

Most people involved
Were only distressed.
An ambulance came
To cart off the rest.

All this chaos
From a stupid banana,
While taking a stroll
On the streets of Savannah.

And I am astounded,

But I can't overcome,

How dangerous bananas

Have really become!

Digging Ditches

Appointed by the government
To dig a ditch from here to there,
Supplied with but a tiny spoon
To resolve the whole affair.

With only a week to finish the job,
I dared not delay.
So I took the tiny spoon in hand
And started right away.

Frantically, I spooned the dirt,
Onward, I persisted.
I would have rather used a shovel,
But management insisted.

They always do it backward,
Whatever the government controls.
They always do it the hard way,
But that's how authority rolls.

There's cramping in my fingers,
And I can't feel my thumb.
Now, the more I think about it,
My entire hand is numb.

No one knows what it feels like
Digging ditches with a spoon.
I've been at it since this morning
And half the afternoon.

I haven't made any progress
In the mud, the grit, and the grime.
I'm absolutely famished,
And I'm making lousy time.

I won't last much longer,
Anyone can see.
It doesn't take a genius to figure
Digging ditches ain't for me.

Cruel and Unusual Punishment

She lives by the Pacific Ocean
On Hawaii's western shore,
Burdened by an ocean view
That she cannot ignore.

Settling down with a book to read,
And a refreshment in her hand,
An apprehensive time indeed,
Her feet upon the sand.

Hampered by the ocean sound,
So dangerous and deep,
Moments later, she was found
Drifting off to sleep.

Dreaming by the open sea,
Her visions come and go.
A better place she'd rather be
That only she can know.

The beach is not the perfect setting,
It has its share of flaws,
Like back in nineteen seventy-five,
And the Spielberg movie *Jaws*.

The coast is simply one of those places
That's as dreadful as can be.
What a grueling life she faces
Living by the sea.

An ocean view with nothing to do,
A challenge to be sure,
It's surprising how much suffering
Human beings can endure.

A Word to the Wise

I was caught in an earthquake today
Because I didn't open my eyes.
I didn't see it coming at me,
So it caught me by surprise.

I fell out of my shoes and socks.
It rattled my teeth and bones.
It wiped out our cable TV
And disrupted our cellular phones.

I wobbled all over the kitchen floor.
It toppled the dining room chairs.
I bobbled through the bedroom door
And tumbled down the stairs.

It tossed me like a Caesar salad
It flipped me like a flounder.
My mom was lost in all the melee,
But later on we found her.

My father was working during the quaking
Right in the middle of town.
He lost his balance during the shaking
And landed upside down.

It jiggled our crystal chandelier.
It rattled the kitchen door.
It tipped over a glass of orange juice,
Which spilled all over the floor.

A lot of valuable items were lost,
And our home's in disarray.
We never tallied up the cost,
But everyone's okay.

So be on the lookout for earthquakes—
Keep your focus true and steady.
If one is heading in your direction,
You're gonna wanna be ready.

And open your eyes, for goodness' sake,
Just a word to the wise.
You wouldn't want an earthquake
Taking you by surprise.

Doorknobs

There are doorknobs installed
On every door.
We know why they're needed.
We know what they're for.

Though we don't know who
Invented the knob,
Somebody thought of it
And tackled the job.

And now we see doorknobs
Nearly everywhere.
There's one over here,
There's one over there.

There's one for the bathroom.
There's one for the shed.
I've got doorknobs behind me
And doorknobs ahead.

Doorknobs are marvelous.
Doorknobs are dandy.
Doorknobs can certainly
Come in handy.

There's one on the front door.
There's one on the back.
There are so many doorknobs,
It's hard to keep track.

But there is one door
Where knobs don't exist—
A door that has sort of
An interesting twist.

It's a door that spins
But maintains control—
A door that is fastened
To a stationary pole.

It'll let you out.
It'll let you in.
It's a door that doesn't know
Where to begin.

For it has no beginning,
And it has no end.
And that's hard for some people
To comprehend.

But you'll notice when walking
Into certain stores,
There are no doorknobs
On revolving doors.

The Aftermath That Followed

Mr. Snyder drank some cider
To quench a burning thirst.
He drank some other liquids too,
But he drank the cider first.

It was cider that was sweet.
It was cider to his liking.
The extent to which he drank it down
Was altogether striking.

Next he poured some homemade tea
From the pitcher to the glass,
Added merely a touch of sugar
And some natural sassafras.

After drinking all the tea,
He had soda pop for lunch,
Washed that down with lemonade
And some watermelon punch.

He sipped a quart of orange juice
While he was standing there.
A pot of coffee was next in line
As well as I'm aware.

He swallowed water by the kettle
And Pepsi by the pail,
Coca-Cola by the goblet,
And a bucketload of ale.

He took every drink in front of him
And made it disappear.
What happened next to Mr. Snyder
Isn't entirely clear.

But witnesses say, he was on his way
To the bathroom in a hurry,
But ended up the last in line,
Which was quite the reason to worry.

A critical moment soon developed
After all the liquid he swallowed.
We can only imagine what happened
In the aftermath that followed.

When It's Time to Pay the Bill

Nobody really likes it
When it's time to pay the bill.
But everybody has to do it—
Everybody knows the drill.

Too many times, I order lunch
Without the money to spare.
Too many times, I've reached for cash
To find it wasn't there.

But I've discovered a clever way
To pass along expenses.
I run up all the debt I want,
Then avoid the consequences.

I order what I want for lunch,
I don't care about the price.
It's a simple but effective plan,
I don't think about it twice.

They bring my order to the table,
And I eat what's on the plate.
Then comes the unfortunate moment
To pay for what I ate.

So when it's time to settle up,
There's really nothing to it.
I simply pass along the burden,
And this is how I do it.

When they put the bill in front of me,
Expecting me to pay,
I slip it in front of someone else,
And look the other way.

I always wait until no one's looking—
The timing here is key—
Just nonchalantly divert attention
And get the meal for free.

I realize it's cheating.
I know it's wrong, but still.
I defer the cost to someone else
When it's time to pay the bill.

Paper Cut

Reading the newspaper
Is a hazardous routine—
An overall tumultuous
And chaotic scene.

For the edge of the paper
And the way that it's made
Can be sharp to the touch—
Like the edge of a blade.

And it happened to me
On page number two,
As I was reading about
What the market would do.

It sliced my finger
At the outermost extension,
Causing ample bleeding
That required some attention.

If you think I was frightened,
Then you're certainly correct,
Because I had a wound
That needed to be checked.

And with a gash like that
It's only prudent to assume,
That I ended up checking
Into the emergency room.

Where the doctor, the nurses,
And the hospital staff
Sewed up the wound
In a minute and a half.

And I'm showing no signs
Of an allergic reaction
From the paper that caused
This minor infraction.

But I'll have to be careful
From now on when I read,
For a newspaper can be
Precarious indeed.

From now on, I'll go online
To get my information.
That might be safer
Than a paper publication.

Just look at my finger
And believe me, you'll see,
How perilous reading newspapers
Can actually be.

PAPER CUT HALL OF FAME

Show Me Where to Sign

I'm in need of a bigger desk
On which to place my things—
A desk that's fit for royalty,
One that's fit for kings.

One that fits my character,
One that fits my style—
A desk that I can be proud of,
Every once in a while.

I could use a desk with purpose,
One that's advantageous,
One that's reasonably convenient
And not a bit outrageous.

If only my desk was suitable,
And that's the whole objective.
I need one I can use in the office
Where a desk can be effective.

I cannot function as it is.
I have no access to my files.
I've got envelopes in disarray
And paperwork in piles.

This desk can't handle the excess
And all the overflow.
I repositioned the calculator,
And the printer might have to go.

Look at the way this desk was made.
Who authorized this inferior design?
If there's a way to get an upgrade,
Just show me where to sign.

It's way too small to be practical,
And I'm tired of complaining.
My desk needs an overhaul,
And there's little time remaining.

Just fill out the forms in triplicate,
And charge the expense account.
I've explained it to my boss
More times than I can count.

Either take my desk, and make it
As big as they'll permit,
Or make everything on top of it
Small enough to fit.

The Day It All Backfired

I always held the dynamite
While Murphy lit the fuse.
Until the day it all backfired,
And blew me out of my shoes.

My legs were in a tangled mess.
My arms didn't fare any better.
It turned my trousers inside out
And pulverized my sweater.

It rattled every tooth I had.
There were shock waves in my cheeks.
I couldn't talk for eleven hours
Or spit for several weeks.

Not only did it knock me out
And incinerate my hair,
It blew my glasses over here
And my wallet over there.

I went deaf for thirty minutes.
My nose was dislocated.
All this happened in an instant
When the whole thing detonated.

It fractured several fingers.
It mangled one of my thumbs.
Holding lighted dynamite
Is as dangerous as it comes.

I never realized that dynamite
Was so precarious to hold.
It's erratic in its unruly behavior,
And it isn't well controlled.

After all the dust had settled,
Murphy couldn't be found.
Perhaps he ran after lighting the fuse
And never turned around.

But I need to find him somehow
And tell him the wonderful news.
That he'll be holding the dynamite now,
And I'll be lighting the fuse!

The Friendly Skies

Dogs can be friendly
As everyone knows.
Cats are as well,
As their loyalty grows.

Goldfish normally
Show little affection,
But live out their lives
Showing little objection.

Hamsters and gerbils
And turtles can be
The very best friends,
I won't disagree.

But there's one tiny creature
I think you will find
Who'd like to be friendly
With all humankind.

Who'll fly right to you
With precise aviation,
And land on your arm
With no hesitation.

It's the friendly mosquito
I'm talking about—
The one thing I realize,
We can't do without.

A critter so cuddly,
Not the least bit shy,
One that's relentlessly
Waiting nearby.

One that approaches
No fear whatsoever,
One that seems stupid,
But yet, very clever.

And don't try to swat them,
Or you'll scare them away.
They're just being sociable
And maybe someday,

You'll come to find out,
And I think you'll agree,
How friendly mosquitos
Can actually be.

They Need to Build a Robot

They need to build a robot
That does it all for me.
Such a robot does not exist
But could there ever be?

A robot that would exercise,
So I don't have to do it.
A robot that could eat my breakfast,
So I don't have to chew it.

A robot that will go to work,
So I can stay in bed.
A robot I can trust to do
The thinking in my head.

A robot that'll clean the table
And scrub the dirty dishes.
One that does what I tell it to do—
One that obeys my wishes.

A robot that'll wash my clothes
And fold them when they're dry,
Who can mow the lawn when I'm gone
And never question why.

A robot that can work all day,
So I don't have to move.
A robot that the EPA
Would certainly approve.

A robot to complete the chores
And never complain about it.
Could there be one that mops the floors?
Regrettably, I doubt it.

Such a robot does not exist
But could there ever be?
They need to build a robot
That does it all for me.

Irony

I've lost my glasses,
And now I can't see.
It's quite a predicament
That's happened to me.

I've placed them somewhere
That they don't belong,
And I've been searching for them
All day long.

Where it is that I put them,
I cannot recall.
But I would like to find them,
Once and for all.

And if they're not located,
What will happen then?
I need to find my glasses,
So I can see again.

And the sooner I find them
The better I'll be,
And the faster they're located,
The sooner I'll see.

It's important to me
That my glasses are found,
If only I had them
To help look around.

And it's as ironic
As irony can be,
That I need them to find them
In order to see.

Vitamin D

The sun appeared this morning
For all the world to see—
Hovering over the eastern sky,
Brighter than bright should be.

It spent the day way up high
Spreading sunshine down below—
Making it easy for all the flowers
And all the trees to grow.

Then it vanished beyond the horizon
Never to be seen again.
It disappeared when darkness neared,
And that's always how it's been.

And no one knows where it goes,
It disappears without a trace
And we don't know why it leaves the sky,
But that's always been the case.

Then tomorrow brings another sun
To spread some vitamin D,
Which begs the question
I've been pondering—
How many suns can there be?

I THOUGHT THE
D
STOOD FOR DOG!

JoJo's Toes

UH, OH!

JoJo the juggler juggled three oranges,
And not one of them hit the floor.
But JoJo the juggler didn't stop there,
He wanted to do something more.

He took several bowling pins
And tossed them through the air,
Carefully flipping them over his head
As high as he would dare.

After that he surpassed himself
By setting the pins on fire,
Adding another pin for good measure,
Tossing them higher and higher.

Then he juggled some hard-boiled eggs
Without even cracking one,
Added a couple of kitchen knives
Just to make it fun.

He finally grabbed three bowling balls
To attempt a feat so daring,
Right up under the stadium lights
While everybody was staring.

Now JoJo never juggled bowling balls,
Not even once before.
It's not the same as the oranges
He juggled from the store.

Tossing the three of them high in the air
Defying all gravitation,
He had them going for a minute there,
But lost his concentration.

The first one landed down on the floor,
The second one following after—
The audience erupted instantly,
In some uncontrollable laughter.

The third one, however, found JoJo's toes,

Smashing them flatter than flat,

And JoJo quit juggling bowling balls

Not too long after that.

Instant Water

Here we have the latest invention
Sweeping across the land.
Let me have your undivided attention
For the future is at hand.

What we have before us
Has never been seen before.
It's a simple packet of instant water
Nothing less, and nothing more.

Just add water to the powder,
And blend it through and through.
Stir the mixture thoroughly,
And that's all you have to do.

The powder blends with the H_2O,
And instant water is created,
Producing liquid out of nowhere,
And it isn't complicated.

Mix it in an empty glass,
Or a thermos if you like.
It's suitable for a picnic,
And it's perfect for a hike.

Bring it on a camping trip,
Or bring it to the beach.
Bring it almost anywhere
When water's out of reach.

Open the instant water packet
Whenever water is needed.
It's a thrifty resource
When your water's been depleted.

I'm delighted it's available,
After hearing so much about it.
The concept makes me wonder
How we ever got along without it.

If you ever find you're out of water,
There's no need to fear—
You'll never have to be thirsty again,
For instant water is here!

A Bunch of Notes

Music has a certain flavor,
And it has a certain groove.
It makes you want to swing and sway—
It makes your body move.

Music makes you tap your feet,
It makes you clap your hands.
There's something cool about it
Everybody understands.

It forces you to keep the rhythm,
And to try and sing along.
It puts a bunch of notes together
Right where they belong.

It's clearly indiscriminate,
It sparks the inner soul.
Music is what makes the youth
Completely lose control.

It motivates your parents
To dance across the rug.
It electrifies the elderly
Like some astounding drug.

Without it, there's an empty space
That nothing else can fill.
There's something found in music
You won't find in any pill.

It nourishes your conscience,
It stimulates your core.
Music seems to fill a void
Like nothing has before.

When you're feeling brokenhearted,
Like so many people do,
Music seems to know exactly
What you're going through.

In the very best of times,
Yesterday included,
Music is for everyone,
And no one is excluded.

Even in unhappy times,
It understands your sorrow.
Music does the same today
As it will do tomorrow.

Thirty Seconds Flat

If someone suffers
From a broken heart
This is what you do:
Take the broken pieces
And a fair amount of glue,

Stick the pieces back together
Like they were before,
Then the heart that fell apart
Won't be broken anymore.

It's a common operation,
A simple one at that,
And that's how you mend a broken heart
In thirty seconds flat.

Chili Peppers

I bit into a chili pepper,
Then began to chew,
And found out very quickly
It was not the thing to do.

My tongue was burning like a fire
My face was turning red,
And I suddenly felt a warm sensation
Steaming through my head.

I spit it out, and now I know
One thing I never knew,
That biting into chili peppers
Is not the thing to do.

Oceanic Panic

I was underneath the water
In a diving suit I wore.
I was there conducting research
Along the ocean floor.

I was down about a mile below
The Mediterranean Sea
With a crew up on the surface
Waiting there for me.

While collecting bits of sediment,
I looked around to see,
Terror from the ocean depths
Now surrounding me.

A man o' war was on the prowl
And floating by my side.
An octopus was closing in,
And I had nowhere to hide.

Right away, a manta ray
Made its presence known,
And soon a swarm of jellyfish
Was in the danger zone.

Orcas came from over there,
I had swordfish drawing near.
What would cause all these creatures
To suddenly appear?

Sharks were swimming overhead,
Barracuda everywhere.
Electric eels were awfully close
And I was running out of air.

I was in a world of trouble
And I was quite concerned.
I had commotion all around,
No matter where I turned.

But the danger at the moment
Didn't matter anymore,
I had to use the bathroom
Like I never have before.

I'm the Janitor Now

I know that I'm the janitor now,
And a janitor is what I'll be.
I'm holding a broomstick in my hand
As you can plainly see.

I wonder what its purpose is
And its mode of operation.
It's the first one I've ever used,
So I'll need more information.

I'm curious as to how to operate
This complicated machine.
It's the most eccentric contraption
I believe I've ever seen.

The procedure isn't very clear,
And it's causing aggravation.
I think I need an expert here
To direct this operation.

It looks a little convoluted.
I need a blueprint, it would seem.
Its function isn't known to me—
It's a complicated scheme.

If I'm supposed to sweep the floor,
I better figure out the routine:
The approach and maybe a little bit more,
And everything in-between.

And if I stick with it long enough,
I'll achieve janitorial status,
But right now I need to figure out
How to start this apparatus.

Rain Glasses

I wear glasses in the shining sun
To cover up my eyes,
To shield them from the UV rays
Of mostly sunny skies.

Made to latch around my ears
And sit on top of my nose,
They function as they always do
And match my goofy clothes.

I wear the kind that fit my face
And protect my hazel eyes.
I own them by the dozen,
Every form and shape and size.

Sunglasses, I have plenty of,
For every sunny endeavor,
But I don't own any rain glasses,
Nor do I know that I'll ever.

Whenever I'm Awake

I dream of thoroughbred horses,
I dream of a grand estate,
Somewhere in a ritzy neighborhood
With a private iron gate.

I dream of being pampered,
And I dream of caviar.
I dream of a lavish limousine
Or some exotic car.

I dream of elegant apparel
And fine imported wine.
I dream of oceanfront real estate
That one day will be mine.

I dream of owning private jets
Or a luxurious super yacht.
I dream about the simple things,
The things I haven't got.

I dream of owning stocks and bonds
And expensive diamond rings.
It's only when I'm sleeping
That I dream these sorts of things.

And I also dream of sitting down
To a hundred-dollar steak.
How come I can't have these things
Whenever I'm awake?

An Apple a Day

I picked an apple from the tree
Where the branch was hanging low.
It had to be the sweetest apple
That a tree could ever grow.

I opened wide and took a bite.
And instantly realized
That the apple I had bitten
Was completely compromised.

That's because this apple contained
Only half a worm—
The kind of worm that likes to wiggle,
The kind that likes to squirm.

All of a sudden it occurred to me
Exactly what I was doing.
The other half of this wiggling worm
Was in the part that I was chewing!

There's nothing wrong with apples
And yes, I like them fine,
But apples having worms inside
Is where I draw the line!

A Mean Guitar

Kembley plays a mean guitar.
He sings a decent song.
He does it with a passion,
But gets the lyrics wrong.

You can hear him through the window.
You can hear him from afar.
You can hear him singing merrily
And playing his guitar.

Melodies in the bathtub,
I listen to him strumming—
Echoes from the bathroom
Bouncing off the plumbing.

Downstairs in the basement,
Upstairs in the attic,
Effortlessly singing—
But the lyrics, problematic.

Riding on the elevator,
His best guitar in tow.
He still can't seem to figure out
How the words should go.

High up on a Ferris wheel
On the fairgrounds in September,
Happily singing loud and clear
The words he can't remember.

Listen close, and you can hear him
Out on the ocean blue,
Getting verses out of order
In a hollowed-out canoe.

Kembley likes to sing his songs
In his own peculiar way,
But struggles with it lyrically
When he decides to play.

Kembley plays a mean guitar,
He sings a decent song.
He does it with a passion,
But gets the lyrics wrong.

Doesn't Matter to the Yak

High up in the Himalayas
Near a dilapidated shack,
Standing there just eating hay—
The one and only yak.

You can offer him some sedge grass
As a dietary snack.
He'll just stand there eating hay—
Doesn't matter to the yak.

You can try to tip him over
In an ill-advised attack.
He'll just stand there eating hay—
Doesn't matter to the yak.

You can order him to draw the plow
Down the field and back.
He'll just stand there eating hay—
Doesn't matter to the yak.

You can recite the monthly forecast
From the *Farmer's Almanac.*
He'll just stand there eating hay—
Doesn't matter to the yak.

You can try and act like him,
But you won't have the knack.
He'll just stand there eating hay—
Doesn't matter to the yak.

If you would rather leave than stay,
Then go ahead and pack.
He'll just stand there eating hay—
Doesn't matter to the yak.

Doesn't matter what you do,
Or say behind his back.
He'll just stand there eating hay—
Doesn't matter to the yak.

For as high as hay can be a stack
He'll just stand there eating hay.
Doesn't matter to the yak, you see,
He does it every day.

Eating hay is protocol,
So you shouldn't be surprised.
Doesn't matter to the yak at all,
As you've probably surmised.

Flying Trapeze

I was swinging along
On the flying trapeze,
Hanging upside down
By the back of my knees.

I was catching the girls
With the greatest of ease,
And passing them over
To another trapeze.

I caught nine altogether,
With one more to go,
While the crowd looked on
At the synchronized show.

The last one sprang
In my general direction,
Our fingertips met,
And we made the connection.

One minute she's there.
Next minute she's gone.
She remembered the stunt,
But forgot to hold on!

The Perfect Spot

I wanted to go and live on the moon
Where nobody else could find me,
And never look back upon the Earth,
So nothing would ever remind me.

I had to leave without a trace
And make it a smooth transition.
I had to alter my physical space
And change my current position.

I wanted to move where nobody else
Was ever willing to go.
I wanted to live in a secret place
That only I would know.

I found a place on the moon
And moved there right away—
A splendid location next to a crater
Where the view is nice and gray.

Where the postman never brings the mail,
And no one calls my phone—
It's almost like a fairy tale,
Being here alone.

I like the fact that I'm isolated,
And I like the spot selected.
I do not miss the Earth at all,
Which is about what I expected.

I have what I've always wanted,
And now I'm where I belong.
I finally got the perfect spot
I've been craving all along.

I'm totally satisfied here on the moon,
But there is one thing I miss:
No one on Earth will deliver pizza
Anywhere close to this.

That's Our Weatherman Bob

There goes Weatherman Bob,
Predicting a weather event.
He told us it would be sunny today,
But that's not how it went.

There was no sunshine in the sky
Like he told us there would be.
Instead of that, what do you know?
I had water up to my knee!

He's the same old weatherman
Who was wrong the day before.
I don't think I can trust him
With the weather anymore.

He thinks he's doing a bang-up job,
But I'll tell you what I know:
Bob hasn't made a correct prediction
For three weeks in a row!

He's always been the weatherman
As far back as I can recall,
But I don't think I'll be tuning in
To Weatherman Bob at all.

Every forecast, a disastrous blunder,
But that's our Weatherman Bob.
He's wrong so many times, I wonder
How does he keep his job?

A New Invention

There hasn't been a new invention
To come along in a while.
Someone must have a patent to record
Or a copyright to file.

We're in need of an apparatus
That everyone can use.
If anyone's come up with anything lately,
I haven't seen it on the news.

And the patent office is just sitting there
With nothing at all to do.
They've been patiently waiting to see
The development of something new.

Something that's both cost-effective
And quite easily produced—
A gadget that'll change our lives,
Once it's introduced.

We need a machine that makes it effortless
To do what needs to be done—
One that's better than ten inventions
All rolled into one.

More useful than the telephone,
More important than antibiotics,
More marvelous than a microchip,
More advanced than modern robotics.

We could use a new creation
More substantial than the sail,
More ingenious than the airplane
Or as simple as the nail.

More momentous than a compass
Or a printing press machine,
We need someone to invent something
That no one's ever seen.

The wheel is obviously a superior invention,
But we need something more.
We need an invention to be invented
That's never been invented before.

The Last Place First

I've misplaced my key again,
I can't unlock the door.
I had this happen yesterday
And many times before.

I wish that I could figure out
Where I put it down.
I hope I didn't leave it
On the other side of town.

I've looked up to the ceiling.
I've searched all over the floor.
But where my key has ended up,
There's no telling anymore.

If I could only remember,
But I can't recall the past.
It's exactly where I put it,
Wherever I put it last.

And the last place I investigate
Is precisely where it'll be.
Always look in the last place first,
That seems to be the key.

Gasoline Tank

The price we pay for gasoline
Has gotten out of hand.
It's not what we had visualized.
It's not what we had planned.

Every time we burn our gasoline,
It's money down the drain.
We can't do much about it,
So we usually complain.

But it doesn't seem to help us much
To criticize our situation.
Supply and demand governs the cost
At every filling station.

We could take exception to it,
But it wouldn't do any good.
I don't think they'll lower the price,
Even if they could.

We supply the money,
And they supply the flow.
So we fill our tanks with gasoline,
And on and on we go.

SORRY!

What I Know of Moles

EAVESDROPPER!

The only thing I know of moles
Is that they dig a lot of holes—
Pits and tunnels way down deep—
Around the time we fall asleep.

It sometimes makes me stop and wonder
Why they like to tunnel under.
I know so little of their ways
Or how they like to spend their days.

Or what else they might like to do,
Or what else they like to get into,
Or how many friends drop in for tea,
Or even who those friends might be.

There's nothing more that I can tell,
Which proves that I don't know them well.
I do know they dig lots of holes,
And that is all I know of moles.

DISTURBING!

How People Love Their Flapjacks

WE ARE RATHER SPECIAL!

Usually served at breakfast
With butter and syrup on top,
As one bites into flapjacks
One finds it hard to stop.

The flavor is overwhelming,
It's an undisciplined addiction.
It's a habit-forming, nonconforming,
Incredible affliction.

I could eat a plate of flapjacks,
Even if I was full,
For it's only a plate of flapjacks
That has this kind of pull.

Never will I ever find,
A breakfast so alluring.
The sickness infects my taste buds,
And it's ever so enduring.

I've enjoyed my flapjacks
Since I was just a kid.
No one knows who invented them,
But I'm so glad they did.

I still wonder who's responsible
For this magnificent creation.
It doesn't matter who it really was,
There's cause for celebration.

A tastier feast, to say the least,
Still remains concealed.
If there is a treat that's as yummy and sweet,
It has yet to be revealed.

Funny Bone

Once I hit my funny bone
And found out very soon
That it wasn't very funny,
Like some hilarious cartoon.

I felt a sharp sensation
And unmistakable harm—
A measure of unpleasantness
Went shooting through my arm.

It was purely accidental,
And a majority of the pain
Made a beeline from my elbow
Directly to my brain.

It caused my arm in fact
To go completely numb,
And I couldn't feel a single thing
From my shoulder to my thumb.

It isn't really so comical.
It's actually agitating.
Banging on your funny bone
Is certainly aggravating.

We should change the name
Because it needs to be updated.
And whoever named it funny bone
Should be evaluated.

The Keep-a-Secret Gang

We keep secrets to ourselves
Whenever we appear.
Spread the wonderful news around,
The Keep-a-Secret gang is here.

We don't tell you anything,
So there's no need to pry.
We have good reason to do so,
But we won't tell you why.

When we come knocking on your door,
You had better let us in.
We'll be there by three o'clock,
But we won't tell you when.

We'll spill soda on your sofa.
We'll poke holes in every chair,
Right there in your living room,
But we won't tell you where.

Four of us make up this gang.
We're twice as many as two.
One directs the other three,
But we won't tell you who.

One's a kook, one's a quack,
And one has a certified glitch.
One of us is off his rocker,
But we won't tell you which.

We stick around and badger people
Longer than the rules allow.
There is a way to get rid of us,
But we won't tell you how.

We keep secrets from everyone,
Everywhere we go.
We won't tell you anything,
And that's all you need to know.

The Man Who Makes Wigs Out of Hair

Leave on the light and don't sleep at night

If you value the hair up there.

From under your bed

He'll approach your head

To cut off all your hair.

He waits until dark when dogs like to bark

With his scissors and empty sack.

And when you are sleeping

That's when he comes creeping,

And begins his stealthy attack.

He'll take every bit of the hair he can get.

And will not leave any behind.

And it's rather weird

But he shaves off the beard

Of anyone he can find.

He will not explain why he trims your mane.

It's part of the plan he's scheming.

He'll snip the split ends

From you and your friends

While you people lie there dreaming.

And just like that, in one minute flat,

Your head is completely bare.

Then in a flash,

He'll sell it for cash

To the man who makes wigs out of hair.

I know it's frustrating,

But he'll be there waiting,

And as soon as your hair grows back,

He'll do it again, but you won't know when

He's planning his next attack.

He knows where to find people with hair,
And he'll take all he wants for free.
He'll get what he needs
As the evening proceeds,
But he's not getting any from me!

Mode of Transportation

We take for granted every day
The extraordinary wheel.
It's applied to most machinery
And for rolling, it's ideal!

Long ago someone had the crazy idea
Of creating a better way
Of getting around the neighborhood
On any given day.

They devised a mode of transportation
Unlike anything ever—
Unique for the earliest human beings
And obviously, very clever.

The wheel is now ubiquitous,
On any type of machine.
No one can function without it,
From the pauper to the queen.

The wheel is found on the ground
On tricycles, trucks, and trains,
And anything that flies around,
Like whirlybirds and planes.

The computer and the internet
Both take second fiddle.
The television and the telephone
Are somewhere in the middle.

All of them put together
Will never surpass the wheel.
Where would we be in our daily routine
Without an automobile?

We don't know who invented the wheel,
And we don't know exactly when,
But we have someone smart to thank,
Someone way back then.

Any type of clever invention
That was truly documented,
Has never surpassed the simple wheel
And has yet to be invented.

We couldn't manage without the wheel.
That's why I'm talking about it.
For getting around, it's ideal—
And we'd still be walking without it.

The People from Nowhere

We are the people from nowhere,
And this is where we are.
We're so happy to be here
And we have traveled far.

Obviously, we're from someplace,
But we do not know where.
We do not live over here.
Nor do we live over there.

We don't know where we'll end up.
We don't know where we began.
We don't have an existing address
Or any sort of plan.

We're just happy to be here,
For we have traveled far.
We are the people from nowhere,
And this is where we are.

Roll the Dice

Bury yourself under covers.
Hide your head in the sand.
Paint yourself in a corner,
And do not take a stand.

If cowering is all too common,
And giving up is nothing new,
If throwing in the towel
Is all you ever do,

If this is how you go through life,
Then it's time to reassess.
It's time to turn your life around
And think about success.

No more hiding in the shadows—
That's no way to live.
Get out there and finally give it
All you have to give!

At times it won't be easy—
Life can knock you for a loop,
Like waiting in the soup kitchen
Just to get a bowl of soup.

You cannot waste a minute
On your future nowadays.
Enough of all this lingering,
Enough of these delays.

It's out there for the taking,
You simply have to try.
The time has come for action,
Success is standing by.

So be gone from under covers,
Pull your head out of the sand.
Step out from in the corner—
Opportunities are at hand.

Don't just sit there playing nice
Or twiddling your thumbs.
Sometimes you have to roll the dice,
And take it as it comes.

NOW WE'RE
ROLLIN'!

Leave Everything to Me

I can make things miserable
If you give me half a chance.
I'm trained and well-adapted
To any circumstance.

I have a record I'm proud of,
And I'm not going to be outdone.
I'm here to ruin the moment,
Then laugh at what I've done.

I'm a pop-up thunderstorm.
I'm inconspicuous at first.
I turn pleasant days into gloomy ones
Whenever I'm dispersed.

I wait until the sun comes out
And the festivities to begin,
Then when no one's looking,
I come creeping in.

I can infiltrate your picnic.
I can ruin your parade.
I can alter any plans
Or decisions that you've made.

Thinking about a round of golf
Or relaxing by the sea?
Don't you give it another thought—
Leave everything to me.

I know it's a sunny day
And you've got things to do,
But you're going to need a raincoat
Before the day is through.

Making disasters of sunny days
Doesn't bother me at all.
If you want the day, both dark and gray,
Don't hesitate to call.

I'll be lurking over the horizon,
And this is my proposal:
If you need me to ruin your day,
I'm here at your disposal.

With My Walrus

With my walrus, we play fetch.
He wobbles after the ball.
He rejoices when he reaches it.
He returns it when I call.

He's not especially limber.
He's not particularly spry.
He's as graceful as an iceberg
Or a boulder bouncing by.

He isn't too athletic.
He's as elegant as an ox.
He moves like a bag of fertilizer.
He's aerodynamic as a box.

I wouldn't say he's agile.
I wouldn't say he's nimble.
The coordination he possesses
Wouldn't fit inside a thimble.

He's cumbersome when he moves around.
He's clumsy standing still.
He needs no push to get him moving,
But if he needs me to, I will.

He's floppy with his flippers.
He's a heaping pile of blubber,
But he loves to chase a ball—
A ball made out of rubber.

What a klutz he is, this walrus of mine,
From the tundra to the shore.
He's awkward and uncoordinated,
He's all of these and more.

He's neither fit nor acrobatic
When he wobbles after the ball,
But he rejoices when he reaches it.
He returns it when I call.

Little Do These People Know

I like being stuck in traffic
And staying after school.
I like cleaning millions of leaves
Out of our swimming pool.

When it comes to paying bills,
I'm absolutely thrilled,
And I can't wait to see the dentist
To get some cavities filled.

Folding laundry is fun for me.
It's a bonus to make the bed.
I've always enjoyed moving furniture,
And I love to bump my head.

My family thinks I've lost my mind.
My friends say I'm bizarre.
Little do these people know
How right they really are.

Under the Bridge I Live Beneath

I live in a box under the bridge.
My shirt is ragged and worn.
I don't have any shoes on my feet.
My pants are shabby and torn.

I haven't shaved in many years.
I never brush my teeth.
I keep no regular company
Under the bridge I live beneath.

Rodents call my pockets home.
Insects hide in my hair.
I should probably take a bath
Because there's something in the air.

I have only scraps to eat.
I feel winter drawing near.
I could use a pillow and blanket,
But you won't find them here.

I don't own any stocks and bonds.
I have no bank account,
No portfolio to my name
And have no cash to count.

So I look around and wonder
And try to think as to how
It could ever get better anywhere else,
Than where I'm living now?

The Writer and the Artist

Here we see the writer writing
A story for the ages.
There we see the artist drawing
All the pictures for the pages.

Two harmonious forces uniting
To achieve a single goal.
It's quite a peculiar obsession
That neither can control.

Working separate, yet together,
Simultaneously creating,
A book where one is writing
And the other animating.

And as one is writing frantically
The other draws like mad,
Using up all the pens and pencils
The world has ever had.

The writer drains the pens.
The artist erodes the pencils.
Both of them wearing out
Their specific utensils.

Yes, the writer and the artist
Are proficient in their endeavor.
Sometimes one is witty,
Sometimes one is clever.

Sometimes fingers grow weary.
Other times, hands grow numb.
The writer wears out his fingers,
And the artist strains his thumb.

In opposite corners of the room
They continue their designs,
Frantically drawing different pictures
And hastily writing lines.

The process that they're going through
Is like a preliminary test,
To see which one of the two of them
Does their job the best.

Nevertheless, we're waiting to see
What this book is all about.
Meanwhile, the writer and the artist
Continue to figure it out.

Other Available Works

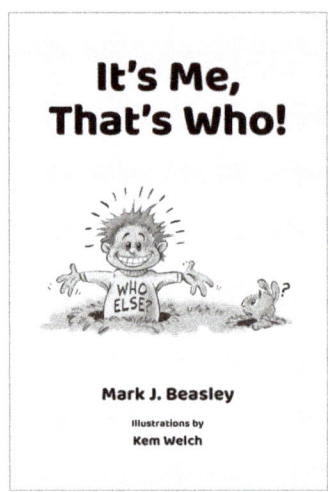

It's Me, That's Who!

Mark J. Beasley

Illustrations by Kem Welch

Mark J. Beasley

HOW HIGH IS UP?

Illustrations by Kem Welch

About Mark J. Beasley

By the age of sixteen, Mark Beasley was writing and cataloging the first drafts of what would become a lifelong endeavor. His first book, *It's Me, That's Who!*, became a reality when a friend introduced him to illustrator Kem Welch. Their ongoing collaboration led to his second release, *How High Is Up?*, and now his third book, *Dragon's Tail for Sale*. The steady progress they've achieved together continues to inspire Mark to write more.

A lifelong resident of Charleston, South Carolina, Mark enjoys motorcycle rides through the Lowcountry and playing bass guitar and singing backup in an original band. He has relatives in Mississippi, Tennessee, and Indiana, and several first cousins in Charleston and upstate South Carolina with whom he spends time. He also enjoys socializing with close friends.